The Friesian Horse

What you need to know if you plan to buy a Friesian horse.

**Written by
Laura Beeman**

The Friesian Horse

What you need to know if you plan to buy a Friesian horse.

Written By: Laura Beeman

Edited By: Joyce Beeman

ISBN 0-7414-0645-4

Cover design by Laura Beeman
Published by:

Infinity Publishing.com
519 West Lancaster Avenue
Haverford, PA 19041-1413
Info@buybooksontheweb.com
www.buybooksontheweb.com
Toll-free (877) BUY BOOK
Local Phone (610) 520-2500
Fax (610) 519-0261

Printed in the United States of America
Printed on Recycled Paper
Published July-2001

To Opal, my first Friesian horse,
your arrival was the fulfillment of a dream.

FOREWORD

Gentle reader, you are in for a delightful tale of a Friesian horse enthusiast's quest for the perfect horse. Laura Beeman set out to write a book introducing the equine shopper to the Friesian horse and has achieved much more. She has created a work that articulates the passion for these noble black horses that all Friesian horse enthusiasts share.

This book contains many beautiful pictures, and a personable penmanship that makes the Friesian horse attainable to you. It explains the FPS books, and clarifies the difference between FPS and other purebred Friesian registries. The history, bloodlines, prices, registration papers and other facts to help you select your perfect Friesian horse are all here.

When I first laid eyes on Laura she was driving her two-year-old filly, Veri, at a fair. The special bond between Laura and her filly was visibly apparent. Veri, with her ears actively listening to Laura, was taking calm, brave steps from Laura's patient voice and hands. She has that effect on me too! Laura is always ready to share her talents and, like the filly, our Friesian chapter has been enriched because of her dedicated support.

Experienced Friesian owners and newcomers alike will find Laura's book a charming, useful addition to their equine library. Enjoy – time and again – the experiences and lessons of Laura's adventure into Friesian horse ownership. To Laura, colleague and friend, thanks for this much-needed book!

Christine Perior
Central California Friesian FHANA Chapter
Shangri La Friesians

PREFACE

I was the child that always rode the black horse on the merry-go-round. As an adult, I owned two beautiful black thoroughbred mares. In the early 1990's, I saw my first Friesian horse. He was magnificent. I felt I had discovered the "ultimate black horse". For the next few years, I conducted research to learn as much as I could about the Friesian breed and saved my money. In 1997, my efforts resulted in the purchase of my first Friesian horse, a ten-month-old filly named Opal. Now, I am owner of Stoney Wood Friesians, a small breeder of registered Friesian horses located in Northern California. We deliver two or three foals each spring and welcome visitors to our ranch by appointment.

At the time I was researching Friesians, it was difficult to find information about this rare breed. With the advent of the Internet and the growth in popularity of the breed within the US, it is significantly easier to find information today.   However, it surprises me that there still appears to be a shortage of written information about the breed. This book is my effort at compiling and providing background information for those of you considering the purchase of a Friesian horse. It is also for those of you, who like me, simply fell in love with them!

DEDICATION

Thank you to my editor and mother, Joyce Beeman, a former English teacher who crosses the t's and dots the i's

Table of Contents

Chapter One

A Brief History of the Breed

The Friesian horse dates back to ancient times and is said to be a direct descendant of the ancient horse, Equus Robustus. The first Friesian horses are believed to have originated in Friesland, a small province in the Netherlands, in the early 16th century. The horse was heavy in build and quite strong. Even so, it was considered to be fairly light on its feet for its size.

During the Dutch Independence war against Spain, the Friesian performed its duties as a war horse. During this time (mid 1500s to mid 1600s), the Friesian was a heavy draft-like breed. Andalusian horses were bred with the Friesians to lighten the body of the Friesian and added to its distinctly animated trot. This resulted in the warmblood Friesian of today.

From war horse, the Friesian changed vocations to become an indispensable partner in agriculture. The strong, hearty constitution of the Friesian made it an excellent horse for performing work on the farm. This was perhaps the introduction of the horse to harness work.

With the mechanization of the farms, the role of the Friesian horse changed once again. Already a well-loved member of the family, the Friesian horse was used to pull the family carriage – to the market or to church on Sunday. Even then, this magnificent horse was appreciated for his beauty as well as his role in the life of his owners.

In the early 1800's Friesians were introduced into sport and became quite popular as trotting horses over short distances. Trotting races were done both on horseback, and in front of a Friesian carriage (*sjees*). These races became very popular in Friesland during this time and the prize for winning the race was often a silver or golden whip. There is still a collection of these whips displayed at the Friesian Museum in Leeuwarden.

Most recently the Friesian horse has become a valued riding horse. The breed is experiencing considerable success as a dressage horse in the United States. Its popularity has grown tremendously in the last two decades, and there are over 8000 registered horses currently residing in the United States.

There has often been controversy around the registration of the Friesian horses, due to the high incidence of cross-breeding. In 1879, the solution was to form two books – the A book for Friesian horses and the B book for crossbreds. Cross breeding became so common that, in 1907, a change was made that would allow the registry of all horses in one book. This could have been a disaster for the Friesian horse and could have caused the loss of the unique breed entirely had it not been for a small group of purists that believed the qualities of the original horse should be preserved. In 1913, these purists created the society "*Het Friesche Paard*" (The Friesian Horse). In 1915, two books were again created. Evaluations were instituted to ensure the breeding of quality horses.

Today, the *Friese Paarden Stamboek* (FPS) is one of the strictest breed registries in the world; and the future of this unique breed has been assured. Within this book, Chapter 4 contains more detailed information about FPS, which is the original Dutch registry from which all modern day registered Friesians originated. In 1979, a German registry, the FPZV, was created. This book is also covered in Chapter 4.

More detailed information about the history of the Friesian horse can be found in the Dutch book, "*Het Friese Paard*" by G.A. Bouma, 1979, printed by Friese Pers Boekerij, bv., in Drachten and Leewarden, the Netherlands. An excerpt from this book is translated into English and provided with permission from the author on the website of the Friesian Horse Association of North America. (www.fhana.com)

The popularity of the Friesian as a riding horse has grown significantly in the last decade in the United States.

Chapter Two

The Bloodlines

All Friesians today are descendants of the stallion Nemo 51. Nemo's offspring went on to populate the entire breed. Today, three primary stallion lines remain, all descended (through many generations) from Nemo. These are Age, Ritske, and Tetman. The Tetman line is by far the largest and is further broken into two major branches: the Jarich line and the Mark line.

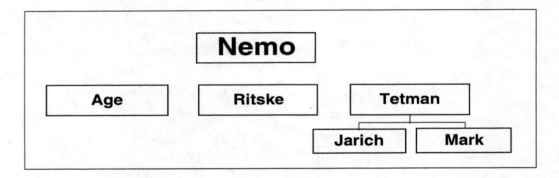

The following pages include some of the detail of each of the three lines. It also details the Jarich and Mark branches. The Mark line produced Hearke, which was such a significant contributor to the breed, that he has his own page as well. These do not reflect all Friesians stallions that ever existed, but do represent the remaining bloodlines that produce the stallions in existence today. (See the appendix for a more detailed chart).

The first line, the Age line is the smallest of the three. At the time of the writing of this book, Lammert is still alive (born in 1975, he is quite old.)

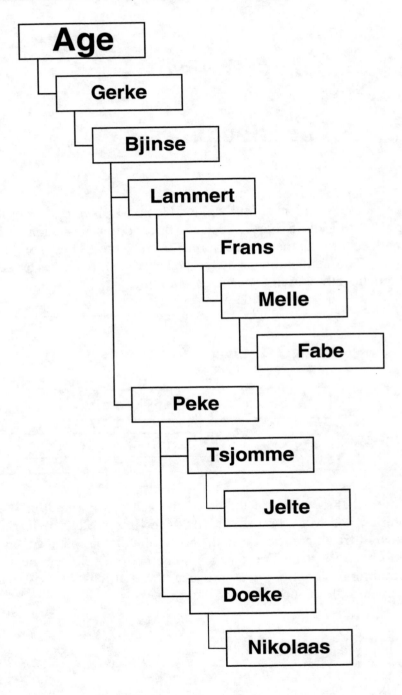

The second line, the Riske line:

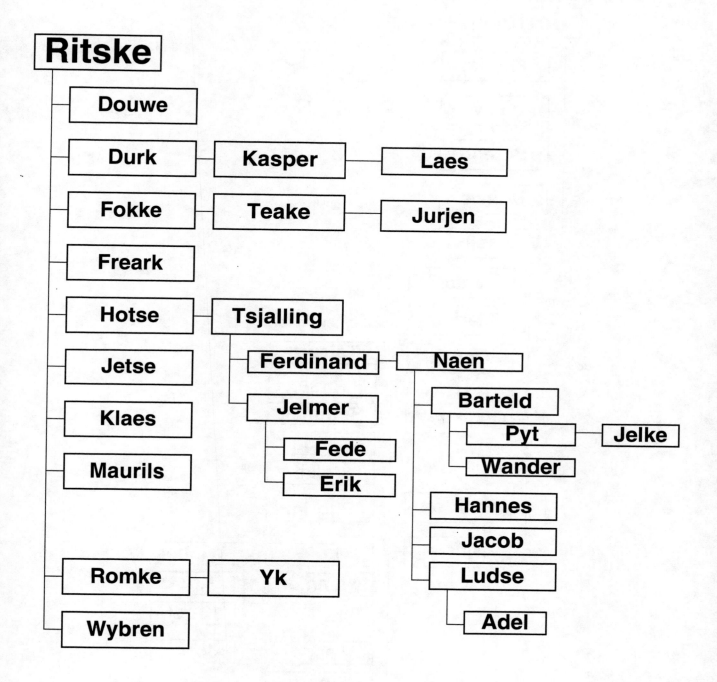

The third line, the Tetman line is further broken into two lines: the Jarich line and the Mark line. This is the Jarich line.

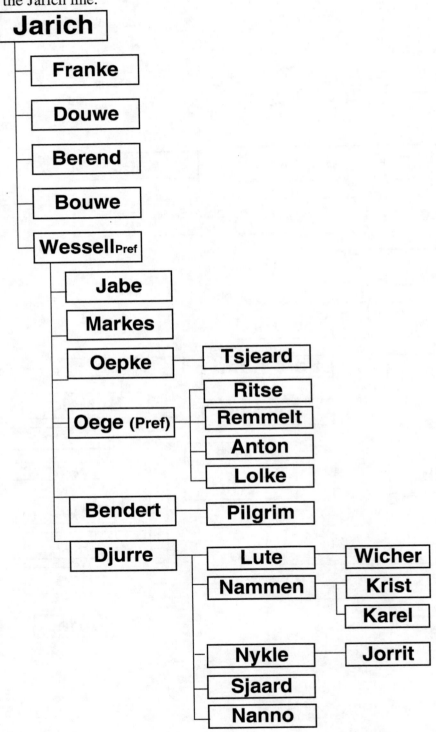

This line is the Mark line. Since it is the largest and most significant, the stallion, Hearke (pref) has been separated into his own line on the next page. He made an outstanding contribution to the Friesian breed and is sometimes said to be the greatest stallion to live during our lifetime.

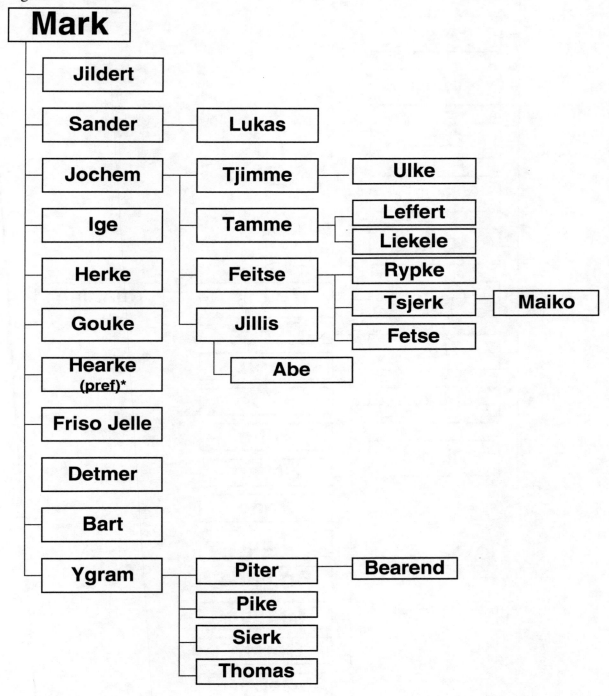

This is the Hearke (pref) line. He was the most famous Mark son.

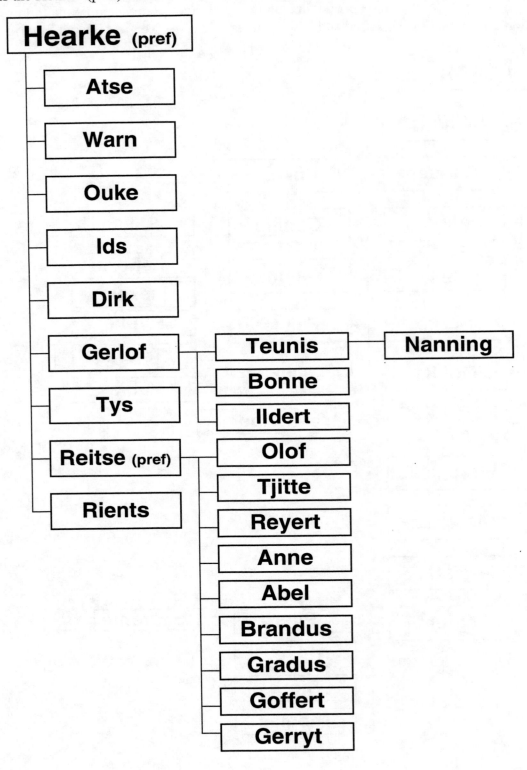

Approved Breeding Stallions

Only approved Friesian stallions may be bred to registered Friesian mares. Offspring resulting from breeding an approved stallion to a registered mare are the only foals that may be registered as purebred Friesian horses. In addition, approved stallions may not breed any other type of mare (i.e.: non-registered Friesian mares or mares of any other breed.)

Stallion Performance Testing

A potential breeding stallion is usually presented to the judges at the keuring when he is 3 to 4 years old. Three-year-old stallions must stand at least 158cm and four-year-olds must be at least 160cm. The judges evaluate the stallions for quality of conformation and gaits, similar to the judging of mares and foals, but the horse must attain a sufficient score and judging committee approval to be allowed entry to the performance tests. The stallion must also pass a detailed veterinary examination, including x-ray evaluation, to gain stallion approval.

A breeding stallion must demonstrate superior athletic ability, have an outstanding disposition and trainability. He must exhibit a wonderful character and heart that shows his willingness to perform. Stallions are required to obtain sufficient scores on all tests. The following chart shows the areas rated for an FPS-approved stallion. These standards have been developed and proven for nearly 100 years in Europe. The purpose of this strict performance testing is to maintain standard criteria for a stallion's performance ability, not just his appearance. Until he can meet these criteria, he is not considered a qualified breeding stallion.

However, the ultimate proof of the stallion's breeding quality is in the foal. Thus, a stallion's approval may be revoked if he is found to be passing on defective traits to his offspring. After a sufficient number of years have passed, each FPS stallion undergoes the evaluation of his offspring. Based on the results of the offspring evaluation, the stallion is either granted the distinction of being "qualified on offspring" or his breeding privileges could be revoked.

Evaluation of Stallions

Walk	Trot	Canter	Riding Test	Driving Test	Pulling Test	Show Driving Test	Character	Stable Behavior	Trainability
6.5	7.5	7	7.5	7	7	7.5	7.5	9.5	7.5

These are the scores for the approved stallion, Nanno 372, who was approved in 1999, and is located in the Netherlands.

FPS-Approved stallion, Pyt, son of Barteld stands in the United States
(Photo courtesy of Pippa Koster and Ghost Ranch in Phelan, Ca.)

FPS-Approved Breeding Stallions in the United States (January 2000)

NAME	BORN	HEIGHT	SIRE	DAM
Bearend 347	June 1992	1.60 m	Piter 312	Sascha 1780 *
Bendert 281	May 1981	1.60 m	Wessel 237 Pref.	Odina 6444 *
Bonne 341	April 1992	1.59 m	Gerlof 294	Gertruda 7879 *
Djurre 284	March 1982	1.64 m	Wessel 237 Pref.	Wijkje 5518 PM
Frans 289	April 1983	1.63 m	Lammert 269	Pauline 6447 *
Gerlof 294	April 1984	1.63 m	Hearke 254 Pref.	Hedrina 6648 *
Laes 278	April 1975	1.63 m	Kasper 229	Vinola 5538 *
Ludse 305	April 1986	1.64 m	Naen 264	Anke S. 7177 *pref
Lukas 324	May 1986	1.61 m	Sander 269	Aaf 6734 *
Melle 311	April 1987	1.60 m	Frans 289	Woltje 6981 *
Ouke 313	May 1988	1.62 m	Hearke 254 Pref.	Erka 5820 * pref
Pilgrim 336	January 1988	1.61 m	Bendert 281	Fokel 7827 *
Pyt 325	May 1988	1.67 m	Barteld 292	Clazien 6734 *
Tjimme 275	March 1979	1.64 m	Jochem 259	Tjimkje 5472 * pref
Wander 352	June 1991	1.63 m	Barteld 292	Nylke S. 9179 *
Warn 335	March 1991	1.62 m	Hearke 254 Pref.	Mefrou 9072 *
Wicher 334	February 1991	1.61 m	Lute 304	Wealtsje 6995 MP

FHS-Approved Breeding Stallions in the United States (January 2000)

STALLION	BIRTH DATE	SIRE	HEIGHT (cm)	YEAR Approved
Aswyn van de Pluum	5/81	Naen	166	1987
Bouwe	3/92	Ids	163	2000
Donius W	3/93	Barteld	162	1998
Drummond	5/93	Jillis	162	1999
Foster v V	3/93	Aswyn vd Pluum	160	1997
Ingram B	9/94	Lute	166	1998
Jan	6/85	Lammert	160	1997
Jorrit	8/85	Mark	162	1997
Laes	4/86	Tsjalling	163	1997
Thor	5/90	Laes	163	1997
Tim	4/93	Dirk	166	1999
Tinus PM	6/90	Jillis	166	1999
Tjerk	4/90	Djurre	161	1999
Tys	5/90	Gerlof	162	1995
Yk	3/91	Romke	167	1995

FHS-Approved Breeding stallion, Jorrit ridden by Sabine Schut
(Photo courtesy of Daisuke Schneider and Proud Meadows Farm in Texas)

FPS-Approved stallion, Wander
(Photo courtesy of Checkerboard Farm in California)

Note: There is a detailed stallion chart located in the appendix which was produced by the Friesian Horse Association of North America and is updated each year with the new stallions that are approved. It is very accurate until the point that the FPZV began approving stallions separately, at which time those stallions were not reflected on the chart. Each year this chart is updated with the newly-approved FHANA stallions.

Chapter Three

Breed Characteristics

In ancient times, Friesians were more draft-like in appearance and were probably truly a cold-blooded horse. However, there has been the infusion of blood from other breeds and today, the modern Friesian is considered a warmblood horse. The body type of the modern Friesian has lightened. Today, most people consider that there are two or three types of Friesians – light, medium and heavy. The lighter horses are sometimes referred to as the "sport horse" or "luxury models", whereas the heavier types are often called the "traditional" or "Baroque" type of horse. Judges should not be biased as to type as long as the horse has good conformation and quality movement.

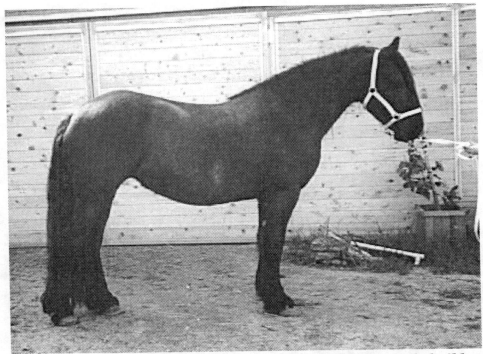

The "traditional" Friesian, has a powerful chest and sturdy build.

Friesian horses are typically 15.1 to 16.1 hands, although there does appear to be a trend toward a slightly taller horse nowadays; and many of the approved stallions are taller. Below is a chart of the minimum height requirements for each type of Friesian horse. A conversion chart that converts centimeters into hands can be found in the appendix of this book.

Minimum Height Requirements per the
Friesian Horse Association of North America

Studbook Mare/Gelding	150 cm	14.3 hands
Star Mare/Gelding	155 cm	15.1 hands
Model Mare or three-year-old approved stallion	158 cm	15.2 ½ hands
Four-year-old approved stallion	160 cm	15.3 hands

There are several common breed characteristics that can be found in most Friesian horses. Perhaps one of the most stunning is the beautiful neck: the neck is upright and crested with a graceful arch and a narrow throat latch. The head is more refined than many of the other draft breeds; and small, alert ears with tips that point slightly inward are desirable. The body of the Friesian should be compact and strong with good bone in the legs and strong, clean joints. Most have rounded withers, and a long, sloping shoulder is desired. Friesians also tend to have strong, solid hooves.

Most notable about the Friesian horse is its beautiful hair. The breed is famous for its long, flowing mane and tail, which have wavy, and sometimes curly, hair. The fetlock area is covered with an abundance of hair known as "feathers". Friesian purists will tell you never to cut the mane, tail, or feathers of your horse – to allow them to grow and have natural beauty. Sometimes this has even meant the absence of a bridle path – which can be quite messy and impractical!

Typical Friesian characteristics include: high neck set, low tail set, abundant mane, tail and feathering on the legs. The well-known Friesian knee action occurs naturally.

FHS-Approved Friesian stallions, Doktor and Tjerk
(Photo courtesy of Proud Meadows Farms in Texas)

In previous times, the Friesian horse came in colors other than black; but, through careful breeding, the modern Friesian has been limited to black only. The modern Friesian horse is prohibited from having any white on its body anyplace other than the forehead. If a horse is produced with white on the body, legs, or feet, it is not permitted in the registry. Some Friesians do carry what is known as the "chestnut gene". This is avoided in Approved stallions. This gene throws a red color and occasionally a chestnut Friesian is born. Because they are unique, the chestnut horses may be entered into the Friesian foal book, but are never granted entry into the studbooks as adults.

While all registered Friesians are considered "black", there are many shades and hues of black. Horses may vary from a warm brown, to a deep midnight blue-black and many even dapple in the summer. There is much discussion about the color of this black horse. Many owners strive to keep their horses as dark as possible by supplementing their food with additives to darken the coat, restricting them to turn-out only in evenings or keeping the horses blanketed at all times. All these measures are purely for cosmetic benefit as the Friesian horse will darken at least twice a year: when it sheds out its long winter coat in Spring, and when it grows its new winter coat in the Fall. These are the times of year when the horse is naturally at its darkest.

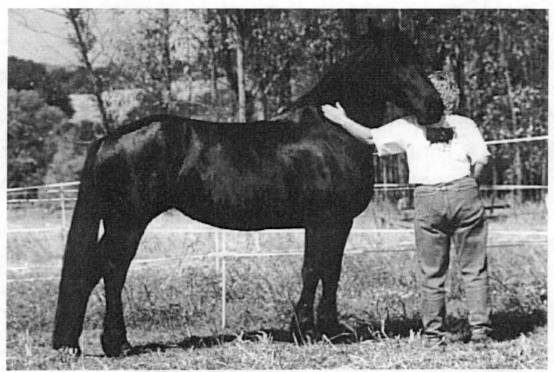

His kind temperament makes the Friesian horse a welcome member of the family.

Perhaps the most outstanding single characteristic of the Friesian horse is its kind temperament. Friesians are very people oriented. They are friendly, willing, and loyal. In general, they make a considerable effort to please and have the ability to retain knowledge. The Friesian horse embodies the quality that horse lovers describe as "heart".

Few other breeds elicit the same kind of immediate passion as the Friesian. People find it incredible that this massive, strong horse is so willing and gentle. There is a kindness in the eye that every horse trainer loves. The Friesian horse can develop a very strong bond with his owner or handler. Perhaps this is why it is so difficult to find trained adult horses for sale. Once a person has invested his time, energy, and heart into a Friesian horse, it's hard to let them go.

Another endearing quality of the Friesian horse is its love of water. You can think of the Friesian as the "black lab of the horse world". Whether it's splashing in puddles in the pasture, pawing in the water trough, or swimming in a lake, these horses just can't get enough water! Needless to say, crossing a stream on a trail ride opens new possibilities with a Friesian – keep him moving or he may just lay down in it!

The "Riding-type" Friesian has plenty of reach in the trot.

Movement

With roots as a trotter, one would naturally expect that the Friesian horse would have a strong, powerful trot. This is generally true, although horses may vary as to their movement. Some horses have more of a lifting of the knees in front which appears very flashy when they are in front of a cart. Other types have the ability to "reach" with the front legs to lengthen the stride of each gait. The type of movement you choose in a Friesian is a matter of personal preference. Although sometimes referred to as the "riding type" or "driving type", many Friesians are able to succeed equally well at both.

A driving horse must have a very elastic trot. He must possess the ability to trot very slowly, at a medium speed, or quite briskly (trot-on!) Very rarely does the driving horse need to canter, and many "driving-type" Friesians have some difficulty with balance when first learning this gait.

The Friesian is most well known for its work in front of the carriage.

The Friesian riding horse must be equally capable and strong at all three gaits. The fact that the Friesian horse is making major inroads into the dressage community demonstrates that this breed is capable of performing under saddle as well. In choosing a Friesian horse, it is important to determine what type of activities he will be asked to perform. Other than extreme endurance riding and extensive jumping, the Friesian horse is a very versatile animal. In addition to driving and dressage, Friesians make excellent trail horses. They are level headed and not likely to spook unnecessarily. In addition, one may choose a Friesian for saddle seat or side-saddle riding, for vaulting, or therapeutic riding. Their calm and deliberate manner makes them an ideal choice for many equestrian disciplines.

The unique characteristics of the Friesian horse make it different from any other breed available today. Coupled with its tremendous beauty and willing character, it is not surprising that the Friesian has become the "Horse of Dreams" for many people.

The Friesian is proving itself as a viable competitor in the dressage ring.

The Friesian horse has a great affinity for water.

Chapter Four

The Friesian Registries

In the Friesian world, it is not uncommon to hear the question "What is a Real Friesian?" In fact, there are two Friesian registries. The first is the FPS which is the original Friesian registry in Holland, also known as "The Dutch Book". The North American representative of this registry is the Friesian Horse Association of North America (FHANA). At one time all Friesians were registered with the FPS.

Later, a group of Friesian owners that were dissatisfied with the methods of evaluation used by FPS decided to start their own registry: the FPVZ which is also known as the "German Book". The American chapter of this registry is the Friesian Horse Society. (FHS) Originally, all horses in both books came from common ancestors; however, FPZV now has its own criteria for approving stallions that are NOT approved by FHANA. So over time, some change may occur in the types of horses in each registry.

This chapter will give a brief overview of each registry as well as a description of how the registries differ (provided, with permission to include here, by the FPZV.) Horses that are not registered with FPS or FPZV are not considered purebred Friesian horses and their offspring cannot be registered as Friesians.

Friese Paarden Stamboek (FPS). – The Dutch Registry

Friese Paarden Stamboek (FPS) is recognized as the European Mother Studbook of the Friesian Horse and is the world-wide authority on the Friesian Horse. The FPS (of which FHANA is the recognized North American representative) is the original Friesian studbook founded in 1879 in the Netherlands. As of 2000, the FPS had about 8,000 members in more than a dozen countries and approximately 30,000 horses registered. The largest numbers of FPS-registered horses are in The Netherlands and Germany, followed by North America. FPS has four major studbooks: the Foal Book, the Mare Studbook, the Gelding Studbook and the Studbook for Approved Stallions. Technially there are other subsidiary registries (i.e.: the B Book) however, the four books listed above are the primary registries.

Breeding Friesian horses within the FPS Studbook System is strictly controlled. A foal can only be registered in the Foal Book register of the main studbook if its dam is in the main studbook (Mare Studbook or Foal Book) and was bred to a studbook stallion with FPS-approved breeding privileges (an Approved Stallion). As of 2001, there are approximately seventy-five (75) such stallions available for live cover or artificial insemination in the world.

The chances of buying a Friesian colt for eventual use as a stallion and having him approved for breeding are very small. There is no category for stallions that have not been approved for breeding. A male horse must either be approved, gelded, or remain in the Foal Book.

Within each Registry, there is further delineation between horses. For example, within the Mare Studbook, there are studbook mares, star mares and model mares. The top horses listed would usually be more costly than the second, and so forth if age, soundness, reproductive status, and similar factors are equal. For example, you would expect to pay more for a Model Mare than a Star Mare, more for a Star Mare than a Studbook (normal) Mare, and more for a Studbook Mare than for one that could not be promoted from the Foal Book to the Studbook (because of a white leg marking, chestnut color, or some physical deficiency, for instance).

Foals, yearlings and two-year-old mares, star mares and geldings can receive premiums (in Dutch: *premie*) when they are judged. On judging day, a first-premium horse demonstrated better movement and conformation than a second-premium horse, which demonstrated better movement and conformation than a third-premium horse. Among adult horses, only Approved Stallions, Star Mares and Geldings, and the best quality studbook mares and geldings are eligible to receive premiums. In the case of multiple premiums, the most recent is the most important.

NOTE: For additional information concerning FHANA rules and regulations, please see the contact information provided in the appendix to this book.

Friesenpferde-Zuchtverband - FPVZ
The Friesian Horse Breeding Association in Germany

Note: Information for the following section was provided FHS — the American representative of the Friesenpferde-Zuchtverband (FPZV) registry. (The German Book)

In 1979, the "Society of Breeders and Friends of the Friesian Horse" was founded in Germany. The society's goal was primarily to promote breeding of purebred Friesian horses in cooperation with the Dutch studbook (FPS), as well as making the breed more popular in Germany.

During the first years, the association organized only one stud show a year in which horses were judged by the FPS commission and were registered in the studbook of Holland.

Besides the systematic organization of the breeding, the FPZV has tried to draw more attention to this rare breed in Germany. Friesians were presented on the EURO-CHEVAL at Offenburg in 1980 for the first time, and the audience reacted enthusiastically. After the presentation of the Friesian horse in 1981 at EQUITANA at Essen, people were fascinated by this outstanding breed. During the following years, the Breeder's Association experienced a large growth in membership. As well, the Friesian horse was most successful at many horse shows and presentations.

As a result of their popularity, the value of the Friesian horse increased on the trade market. More and more people also wanted to help the breeding process. Because of federal laws, the "Society of Breeders and Friends of the Friesian

Horse" had to prepare new criteria and registration procedures in order to make an organized breeding of Friesian horses possible. The Society was renamed the Friesian Breeders' Association.

Friesenpferde-Zuchtverband e.V, (FPZV) and the new regulations were adopted. The new registration orders and the studbook were accepted by the state after a government-appointed breeding director was chosen. This allowed FPZV to apply for membership in the German Federation Nationale or "FN", a national association for all horsemen. With both FN and state approval, FPZV became an independent breeding organization in Germany.

Since then, the number of Friesian horses in Germany and, therefore, the number of members of the FPZV has increased steadily during the years. Successful work has increased the interest of other nations resulting in foreign breeders joining the FPZV and in the development of affiliated organizations like FHS in the United States, which was established in 1993. Today the FPZV is internationally active in breeding as well as in sports, and the organization continues to grow.

For additional information concerning FHS rules and regulations, please see the contact information provided in the appendix to this book.

What is the difference between FPZV and FPS ?

The Friesian horse is evaluated on performance.

Note: Information in the following section was provided with permission from FPZV.

The Germans applaud the Dutch for their perseverance in the preservation of the breed. The Germans maintain exactly the same criteria in judging the conformation of the horse and feel there is no need to change or alter what the Dutch have developed as the recognized standards of the Friesian breed.

However, there are three major differences between the Dutch and German requirements: (1) judging of the movement of the horse, (2) mare performance testing, and (3) the allowance of cross-breeding. Although the judgment of the quality of the movement is similar to FPS, in that FPZV counts quality of the movement as 60% of the total score of the horse. However, there is a difference with regard to how the movement is scored. Each of the three basic gaits is not weighted equally in the score by FPZV, as it is with FPS. Scores for walk, trot, and canter are multiplied by factors of 1.2, 1.0, and 0.8, respectively. Training can improve what is often the most difficult gait for a Friesian: the walk. One should expect this to be the most difficult gait particularly for foals to do well, since they have not had training. Thus, if a foal has a correct, ground-covering walk with lots of action, it is rewarded for this natural tendency with the "bonus" score (score X 1.2). Most Friesians, foals included, have a naturally beautiful trot so this is scored more neutrally (score X 1.0). The canter is weighted less heavily because it is considered easy for the Friesian, who normally possesses a ground-covering, elevated canter (score X 0.8). These differences are reflected in the philosophy of the Germans as they relate to the future of the Friesian horse. They believe that for the Friesian to retain and advance its status in the horse world, the Friesian must be able to compete against all the world's great horse breeds.

Gait	Multiplication Factor
Walk	1.2
Trot	1.0
Canter	0.8

For this horse to be competitive, it must be forward-moving. This trait is natural for some Friesians. The Germans, from the inception of their breeding association, have maintained this standard in the selection of its approved Stallions. The results of this careful selection has resulted in the development of very good pleasure horses and highly-competitive sport horses. The German view is that the Friesian is capable of becoming a highly-competitive performance horse, which will insure the expansion of the market for the Friesian horse.

As leaders in the world of equine sports, the Germans' uncompromising search for the selection of the best horses is a matter of national pride. Evaluation criteria extend beyond the Stallions to the other half of the foal — the mare. To attain the honor of Star or Model in the FPZV registry, the mare must also pass a performance test in dressage and driving. Although both associations have similar philosophies about mare testing, the rules are more strictly adhered to regarding this particular item by FPZV. According to 1998 FHANA rules, to earn the designation "Star" (Rule 3.3.2.3), "mandatory IBOP testing, or the equivalent, may be required." For "Model" (3.3.3.4) "the mare must pass an IBOP performance test. Performance ability may be proven under saddle or as a driving horse." This testing requirement, hasn't always been enforced by FHANA especially for "Star" mares. Under current FPZV rules, however, mare performance testing for "Star" or "Model" is an absolute requirement prior to the mare's achieving this honor. Tests in both dressage and driving are required. This comprehensive search to develop the finest of the Friesian breed will result in a horse that we can all be proud of in the 21st Century!

What about cross-breeding?

The cross-breeding of Friesians has been in practice for centuries, influencing the development of various other breeds. These include several pony breeds in Great Britain, most notably the "mini-Friesian" or Fell pony which originated in Roman times. Friesians brought to North America in the late 18th Century were literally cross-bred out of existence. They were reintroduced in the 1970's. That early Friesian blood is believed to have influenced the development of several North American breeds, including the Morgan and Tennessee Walking Horse.

Because of the previous danger of losing the uniqueness of the Friesian horse, the FHS (Dutch) prohibit any cross-breeding (mares or stallions) and approved stallions can lose their breeding privileges if they are found to be engaging in this practice. The cross-breeding of Friesian horses is not promoted or encouraged by FPZV either, and the use of purebred Friesian mares for cross-breeding is not allowed. However, FPVZ believes the use of a Friesian stallion for cross-breeding is the decision of the individual owner. According to the current regulations, the FPZV will recognize crossbreeds under the following conditions:

- Stallion must be an approved stallion.
- Mare owner must be a member of FPZV/FHS.
- Mare must be registered by a fully-recognized breeding organization.
- Foal receives a birth certificate and registration in Foal Book II (NOT the Studbook).
- Foal offspring will have no recognition by FPZV.
- Foal must be judged and branded by FPZV.
- Foal must have DNA verification of sire.

There is much controversy over the cross-breeding issue, and many owners of unapproved stallions in the United States choose to "leave the registry" and cross-breed their stallions. This means that other breeds are not breeding to the highest quality Friesian stallions and not necessarily getting the "best of the breed".

Cross-bred colt – Arabian mare by an unapproved Friesian stallion.
(Photo courtesy of Ingrid Smith of the Friesian Forest in California)

Chapter Five

Breeding

Friesian filly in beautiful form at only 5 weeks old

Breeding Methods

Both FPS and FPZV permit breeding by live cover, artificial insemination and embryo transfer. Although regulations concerning the embryo transfer vary for each registry and should be researched thoroughly before embarking on such an involved (and costly) process. Transported semen is very common – both shipped cooled and frozen.

The inbreeding coefficient

Inbreeding coefficients were introduced by the FPS in 1988. This is a numerical score that is computed for the horse based on the re-occurrence of particular ancestors in the pedigree. A low inbreeding coefficient indicates the horse has few common ancestors. The coefficient is provided on FPS registration papers. (See chapter 7 for a sample mare registration paper and location of the inbreeding coefficient.)

Although no strict guidelines are published by FPS that restrict the inbreeding coefficient, in general, a horse with a coefficient of 10 or over is considered quite high. A breeder might strive to keep all foals with coefficients under 5. Today, with the increased availability of stallions due to the use of shipped cooled and frozen semen, it is possible for breeders to target their foals with coefficients under 3.

A breeder can use the inbreeding coefficient as one method of choosing a stallion appropriate to his mare. FHANA offers a service for Dutch registered horses to assist in this analysis. Through the FHANA web site, the mare owner provides the name and registration number of the mare and is then asked to select which FPS stallions they are interested inbreeding to. The computer program then calculates what the inbreeding coefficient would be for a foal conceived by that pairing.

For FPZV registered horses, an owner can manually conduct this same analysis by examining the papers of the stallion and mare and looking for overlapping ancestors in the first four or five generations. A single common ancestor is not unusual and should be no cause for alarm. Multiple overlaps or the repetitive presence of one particular stallion should be of concern.

A Friesian mare and her new foal enjoy a romp in the pasture.

Each year FPS provides the letters that the foal's name must begin with. For example, in the year 2000, all foals were required to have registered names that began with A, B or C. This can be a very valuable practice in quickly identifying the approximate age of a horse based on its registered name. Names of fillies cannot be duplicated in the same year, but colts may. Often a last initial is added to the name to keep it unique. For example, if there were two Marias, one might be named Marie B. (The initial of the last name of the owner is usually used.

Sample Initial Letter Chart

YEAR	LETTER
1995	JKL
1996	MNO
1997	PQRS
1998	TUV
1999	WXYZ
2000	ABC
2001	DEF

Star Mare and young filly.
(Photo Courtesy of Itzen Friesians of Brookings, Oregon)

New-born foal with attentive mother.

Perhaps there is nothing more wondrous than a new foal. By and large, the Friesian mares are excellent mothers. By using the tools and information provided by the registries, it is possible to make intelligent choices about which stallions would best suit your mare and to continue the conscientious effort being made by Friesian owners today to continually improve the breed. The registries are particularly helpful in answering questions and are a great source of assistance for the new Friesian owner that is considering breeding their mare.

Chapter Six

The Keuring

The judges from Holland inspect a three-year-old mare for inclusion in the Mare studbook. Horses are evaluated 40% on conformation.

For the purposes of this book, the process used by the Friesian Horse Association of North America (FHANA) will be discussed. Each registry has its own particular rules and formats for horse evaluation. As a potential Friesian owner, you should review and familiarize yourself with the materials available from each registry

.

A judging (*keuring* in Dutch) is an evaluation of horses here in North America, by officials from the Netherlands. Once a year, teams of officials qualified by the Friesch Paarden Stamboek are sent to North America to inspect or "judge" horses. This is a thorough evaluation process that helps us to upgrade our breeding programs. The horses are judged in-hand: 60% of the evaluation is based on the quality of movement, and 40% is based on conformation.

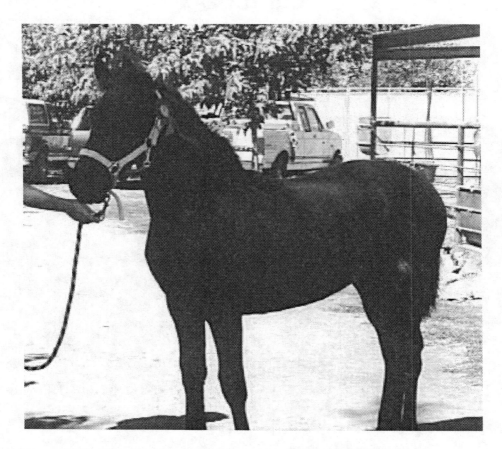

A proud filly displays her red ribbon, awarded for "Second Premie" status. She was shown at her mother's side and entered into the foal book.

Most Friesians are judged twice in their life: once when they are foals—for entry in the Foal Book—and again when they are three years or older and eligible to enter the adult studbooks. Foals must be shown at their mother's side within their first year of life. When a foal or horse is judged, it may be awarded a *premie*, or "premium". This is an award used to designate the horses with the most desirable characteristics. A first premium is best (orange ribbon), second is very good (red ribbon), third is most common (white ribbon). Some horses will not receive a premium and, consequently, receive no ribbon. The premiums awarded to each horse appear on his or her registration certificate.

Premium	Ribbon	Percentage
First	Orange	Top 5%
Second	Red	Next 35%
Third	White	Next 50%
None	None	Last 10%

After the babies are evaluated on the day of the Keuring, the current practice is to have each foal micro-chipped. A licensed veterinarian inserts a tiny microchip into the crest portion of the neck. This chip contains a unique number, which can be used to identify the horse throughout its life. This number is recorded on the horse's papers. In years prior to 1997, a number was tattooed on the underside of the foal's tongue. Papers issued prior to 1997 have the tongue tattoo number instead of the micro-chip number listed. If a horse's papers are lost, it should be possible to correctly identify the individual through the use of the tongue tattoo, micro-chip, and brand indications.

Horses are evaluated 60% on movement at the walk and trot. In addition to the premium, as each mare or gelding is judged for admission to the adult studbooks, it is ranked using a linear score sheet. This linear score assigns positive or negative point scores to many individual aspects of conformation, breed characteristics, and movement as exhibited by the horse. The score sheet for each individual horse is given to the owner. In addition, the linear scores for all the offspring of each stallion are combined and published. This composite score provides a way of evaluating the strengths and weaknesses that each stallion passes on to his offspring. By matching the strengths and weaknesses of the mare and stallion, we can use the linear scores to choose the best match between sire and dam in order to improve the breed continually.

The following pages show the Dutch and English versions of the linear score sheet.

Sample FPS Evaluation Form in English

Place:	Country:	Cat.nr:
Date:	Name of horse:	
Sex: S M G	Reg.nr:	Tonguenr:
Height:	Father:	Mother:
Marking:	Reg.nr:	Reg.nr:

	Mark	5	10	15	20	25	30	35	40	45	Mark
Head	plain										noble
	big										small
Nape of neck	short										long
Head/neck connection	heavy										light
Neck	short										long
	horizontal										vertical
	heavy										poor
Withers	short										long
Shoulder	short										long
	steep										sloping
Back	long										short
	weak										tight
Loins	small										broad
	weak										tight
Croup	straight										slanted
	short										long
Gaskinmuscle	short										long
Length of forearm	short										long
Frontleg(s)	standing over										standing under
	hollow										goatlegged
Hindleg(s)	bowlegged										cowheeled
	sickle hocked										straight
Development of joints	coarse										fine
Pastern	short										long
Hoofs	small										big
Heels	low										high
Quality of legs	spongy										hard
	heavy										fine
	wide										narrow
	toeing-in										toeing-out
Walk	short										long
	irregular										tactfull
	weak										powerfull
Trot	short										roomy
	irregular										tactfull
Movement/impulse	weak										powerfull
	flat										highly lifted
Color	faded black										jetblack
Hair growth	little										much

o dressage-type o show-type	Racialtype	Structure	Muuculation	Legwork	Walk	Trot

o deep from the chest o too heavy lower neck o wrongly formed knee o wrongly formed hock o umbilical hernia o mane eczema	o not registered o studbook o star o provisional model
	Member of the jury:

38

Actual Dutch evaluation form for a three-year-old mare.

Plaats:	Western Circuit	Land:	U.S.A.	Cat.nr:	784
Datum:	22.09.1999	Naam:	Opal		
Geslacht:	Merrie	Reg.nr:	199624120	Tongnr:	FH06T1V
Stokmaat:	156	Vader:	Jildert	Moeder:	Jolanda
Aftekening:	Geen	Reg.nr:	198502991	Reg.nr:	198581970

	Kenmerk	5	10	15	20	25	30	35	40	45	Kenmerk
Hoofd	onedel					X					edel
	lang							X			klein
Nek	kort				X						lang
Hoofd/hals verbinding	zwaar				X						licht
Hals	kort				X						lang
	horizontaal						X				verticaal
	zwaar				X						arm
Schoft	kort						X				lang
Schouder	kort							X			lang
	steil							X			schuin
Rug	lang				X						kort
	week				X						strak
Lendenen	smal							X			breed
	week						X				gedreven
Kruis	recht							X			afhellend
	kort						X				lang
Broekspier	kort					X					lang
Lengte onderarm	kort					X					lang
Voor be(e)n(en)	gestrekt				X						onderstandig
	hol						X				bokbenig
achterbe(e)n(en)	o-benig					X					koehakkig
	sabelbenig				X						recht
Ontwikkeling gewrichten	grof					X					fijn
Koot	kort						X				lang
Hoeven	klein						X				groot
verzenen	laag					X					hoog
Kwaliteit Benen	voos							X			hard
	zwaar				X						fijn
Stap	wijd						X				nauw
	toontredend				X						frans
	kort							X			lang
	onregelmatig							X			tactmatig
	zwak						X				krachtig
Draf	kort				X						ruim
	onregelmatig			X							tactmatig
Beweging/impuls	slap			X							krachtig
	vlak						X				verheven
Kleur	vaalzwart							X			gitzwart
Behang	weinig						X				veel

	Rastype	Bouw	Bespiering	Beenwerk	Stap	Draf
dressuurtypisch tuigtypisch	7,0	7,0	6,5	6,5	7,0	5,5

diep uit de borst onderhals afw. knie afw. sprong navelbreuk manenexceem	opgenomen in stamboek
	Jurylid: Mulder

39

For adult horses, entry into the studbook is reflected by a brand. The current practice is to freeze-brand an "F" onto the left side of the neck of all adult horses entering into the studbooks.

The very best quality adult mares and geldings may be granted additional status. The following additional honors can be granted:
- Star Mare or Gelding
- Model Mare
- Preferential Mare
- Performance Mother

Once status in the studbook has occurred the following requirements are necessary for entry into the other registers.

Star Mare or Gelding: At the time of initial entry into the studbook, mares and geldings are also evaluated for star status. This will only be given to approximately 20% of horses judged and is an honorable distinction. To become a star, the mare or gelding must be a minimum of 1.55 meters (15.1 hands), have totally correct movement, and have conformation that meets the breeding objectives as defined in the applicable registry, For FHS horses, additional performance criteria are required. If the mare or gelding is granted the status of star, an "S" is branded next to the "F" on the left side of the neck.

Model Mare: Once granted the status of star, a mare may be eligible for model mare status. The mare normally be seven years old or more, stand at least 1.58 meters (15.2 ¼ hands) and have born and nursed a foal. She must demonstrate she is among the best of all star mares worldwide by outstanding conformation and superb movement. First, she is granted "Provisional" model status and must then complete a performance test within the next year to prove her capabilities as a riding or driving horse. Model mares are branded with an "M" on the left side of the neck.

Preferential Mare or Approved Stallion: This status is granted to horses that have proven themselves by consistently producing quality offspring. To qualify for preferential status a horse must have a minimum of four offspring that have achieved:

> Star or model mare
> Star gelding
> Studbook stallion
> Stallion that reached the
> 2nd level of stallion judging

The horse is branded with a crown on the left side of the neck.

Performance Mother: This status is granted to mares that have proven themselves by producing offspring that have excelled in performance endeavors. To achieve this honor, the mare must have at least three offspring that achieve high levels of performance as riding or driving horses.

A horse is shown in hand for the judges to evaluate movement at the walk and trot.

Photo courtesy of Cindy Peterson.

Note: To see how the status of the horse is reflected on the papers, refer to Chapter 7 for an explanation of how to read FPS registration papers.

Chapter 7
What You Should Know

How much does a Friesian horse cost?

The price of horses varies considerably and it would be of little value to the potential Friesian owner to have an estimated cost of a horse at the time of the publishing of this book as it would quickly become out-of-date. Instead, the following process provides the potential owner with a method of determining the market value at the time he or she is considering a purchase.

The potential buyer should create a spreadsheet like the one on the following page with defined headings. This format allows for the capture of pertinent information in this process. Some sample data has been entered into this spreadsheet as an example.

By contacting breeders listed with each registry and requesting sales lists, the potential buyer can then "fill in these blanks" to determine what the sales price for particular type of horse is averaging.

The following things should be taken into consideration when determining the value of a horse:
- Weanling foals are typically the least costly.
- Male horses are typically less expensive than females.
- The older the horse, the more costly until the mid-teens.
- Horses already offering saddle or driving training are more expensive.
- Horses with star, model or preferential status are increasingly more valuable, and, thus, more costly.
- Mares in foal are more expensive (two-in-one package).

The resulting chart will help you understand the prices of horses in the Friesian market. The potential buyer will be aware that in a market where weanling foals are selling for $10,000, the advertisement reading "WANTED– Friesian mare, age 5-9 years old, second level dressage, must be under $5000" is never going to be answered.

This simplified method for estimating prices is no substitute for actual knowledge. It is a method to help educate the potential buyer so they will not be shocked by prices or be insulting to a breeder by offering a completely inappropriate price. If unsure about whether the horse is worth the asking price, it is recommended that a potential buyer enlist the assistance of a qualified equine appraiser. Then an unbiased and educated analysis can be performed.

Understanding FPS Registration papers

The following page shows a copy of the actual FPS registration papers for a studbook mare named Allie Bouwina born in 1992. Note the circled numbers above each section of the papers. Immediately following the papers is a description of each section, which is translated and defined.

Example of method for charting current prices of horses

Name	Sex	Age	Height	Training	Sire	Dam	State	Price	Terms
Maaike	Filly	Weanling	N/A	N/A	Nanno	Lucky*	CA	11,000	cash
Femke	Filly	Yearling	14H	N/A	Ludse	Sarah	MN	13,500	Pmts ok
Jillis	Colt	Yearling	14H	N/A	Wander	Wijkje	CA	11,500	cash
David	Gelding	4 years	16H	Rides drives	Brandus	Wilma	NY	18,000	Pmts ok
Jouke	Mare	4 years	15.2H	Rides drives	Nanning	Wanda	NY	22,000	Cash
Rita*	Star mare	6 years	15.3H	Rides Drives	Erik	Marie*	CA	28,000	Pmts ok
Claudia*	Star Mare in foal	7 years	15.3H	Rides Drives Breed	Pyt	Peggy*	CA	35,000	Pmts ok

(1) PS register
Stamboek

(2) geslacht
Merrie

(3) registratienummer
199216470

(4) tongcode
F1ZZTXZ

(5) geboortedatum
21.05.1992

(6) inteeltcoëfficiënt
2,34 %

(7) geregistreerde naam
Allie Bouwina

Kleur Zwart
Aftekening Geen
(8) Brandmerk, linker halsvlak F

1992: 3e premie
(9)

(13) pgenomen
8.09.1995

Schofthoogte 158 cm. 18.09.1995

(10) Fokker
660167 Robert/Amy de Boer 2839 144 th Ave
Dorr., MI. 49323-9708 U.S.A.

(11) Eigenaar
660167 Robert/Amy de Boer 2839 144 th Ave
Dorr., MI. 49323-9708 U.S.A.

(12)

(14) **BOUWE**
197002421 Stb

JARICH
196202281 Stb

Tetman
195602051 Stb

Ewold
194501811 Stb
Minsje
195237420 Stb Ster

LAUKJE
196351800 Stb Ster+Pref

Stienke
195542310 Stb Ster

Lutsen
195101921 Stb
Barber
194323100 Stb Model

Ritske
195502021 Stb Preferent

Eelke
194501831 Stb
Brecht
194323020 Stb Preferent

DAEN
198202861 Stb

Tjits
195642830 Stb Model

Ewold
194501811 Stb
Ietje
194932110 Stb Ster

Jochem
197402591 Stb

Mark
196402321 Stb Preferent
Ottsje
196553400 Stb Ster+Pref

(15) **SARAH ROSE**
198910570 Stb

Lindgerd
197566680 Stb Ster

Dagho
197102471 Stb
Bea
197058220 Stb Ster

JACQULYN
198584280 Stb

Naen
197602641 Stb

Ferdinand
197202521 Stb
Truus
195643160 Stb Model+Pref

Suzanne
197866180 Stb Ster

Hearke
197302541 Stb Preferent
Akke

(16)

(17)
Koninklijke vereniging Het Friesch Paarden Stamboek
Postlaan 1A
9204 WT Drachten
telefoon 0512 - 523888 fax 0512 - 532146

Afgegeven 08.11.1995 Ing. S.H. de Boer, sekretaris

Translation of each section of the FPS Registration Papers

1) FPS registry: This will be one of the following;
Stamboek means "studbook'. There are three books: one each for mares, geldings, and stallions.
Veulenboek means "foal book".
Bijboek mean "B Book" which is a separate registry for horses with restricted backgrounds.

2) *Geslacht* means "sex" and will be one of the following:
Female = Merrie
Male = Hengst

3) *Registratienummer* means registration number.
Starts with the first four numbers of the year born. (ie. 1992)

4) *Tongcode/chipnummer*
In general, prior to 1995, foals were tattooed on the underside of the tongue with this number. In 1995 and after 1995, foals have had or will have a micro-chip implanted in their neck with this number.

5) *Geboortedatum* means "birth date".
It will be listed in the format: day/month/year.

6) *Inteeltcoefficient* means "inbreeding coefficient"
See Chapter 3 for more information on the inbreeding coefficient.

7) *Geregistreede Naam* means "Registered Name".

8) This indicates if the horse has been branded and if so, with what letter (F,S,M)
Schofthootgte means height and it is given in centimeters. (A conversion chart is provided in the appendix which translates this into hands.) Immediately following the height is the date the height measurement was taken, in day/month/year format.

9) This is the history of presentation to the judges. It will have a year, and then rating (i.e. 1992: 3epremie) This means in 1992, this horse received a third premium. Also, the words "*niet gekeurd*" with a year may be displayed. That means "not shown" for that year.

10) "*Fokker*" is the breeder of the horse. To the left of name is the breeder's membership number.

11) "*Eigenaar*" is the owner of the horse (at the time the papers are issued) Prior to the name is the owner's membership number.

12) There may also be another listing just below the Owner that will say "*Staat van overdracht*" which means "transferred by".

13) This is the date which the horse was entered into the studbook, in day/month/year format. Note: On foal papers, it is normal for this to read "not entered in studbook".

14) This is the name of the horses sire (father) and his registration number and status. He could be *Vb, Stb, Ster, Pref.*

15) This is the name of the horse's dam (mother) and his registration number and status. He could be *Vb, Stb, Ster, Pref.*

   Note: The rest of the pedigree is read as follows: Move from left to right. The upper horse listed is the father and the lower is the mother. These papers show four previous generations. (i.e. Sara Rose's sire is* Daen. *His sire is* Jochem *and his dam is* Lindgerd, *a star mare)

16) This is the FPS seal and displays in RED.

This is the signature and validation of the person entering the horse into the FPS registry.

Purchasing a Friesian (FHANA)

At the time the horse is purchased, the seller should provide the buyer with a complete Bill of Sale stating the registration number of the horse and other pertinent selling information. In order for the horse to be transferred into the buyer's name, the buyer must first be a member of FHANA. The seller then has the responsibility to mail the original papers directly back to FHANA, so they may be recorded and re-issued in the new buyer's name. A transfer fee is due at this time, and it is customary for this fee to be paid by the seller – but be sure to clarify this with the seller before you buy.

The fact that the original papers are sent directly into the registry and do not go with the horse can be very confusing for a new buyer that is not familiar with registry practices.

Expect that it will take several months for the papers to be re-issued by the registry.

A Friesian and his owner dress as "Zorro" for a costume class.

Proud Friesian owners riding in a quadrille.

Appendix

A SPECIAL THANKS

Friesian Horse Association of North America (FHANA)
Address: P.O. Box 11217
Lexington, KY 40574-1217
Fax: (541)549-4770
Website: www.fhana.com

The Friesian Horse Society, Inc. (FHS)
Address: 1302 South Duncanville Road
Cedar Hill, Texas 75104
Attn: Cora Boesch, General Secretary
Phone: 972-274-0629
Fax: 972-274-0497
Website: www.friesianhorsesociety.com

REFERENCE MATERIAL

Phryso - a monthly publication from the FPS in the Netherlands written in Dutch. There is also an international version that has three languages.

"His Majesty the Friesian" parts 1 and 2 – a Video tapes series that discusses the Friesian bloodlines. It ends in approximately 1994 so stallions approved by FPS after that, or by FPZV, are not included on this tape.

Friesian Horses by Tomas Micek
1994 by Sunburst Books in London
A brief photo book of Friesian horses with limited text in English

The author's website: www.stoneywoodfriesians.com

Height Conversion Chart

Centimeters	Nearest ¼ inch	Hands
150	59	14.3
151	59 ½	14.3 ½
152	59 ¾	14.3 ¾
153	60 ¼	15.0 ¼
154	60 ¾	15.0 ¾
155	61	15.1
156	61 ½	15.1 ½
157	61 ¾	15.1 ¾
158	62 ¼	15.2 1/4
159	62 ½	15.2 ½
160	63	15.3
161	63 ½	15.3 ½
162	63 ¾	15.3 ¾
163	64 ¼	16.0 ¼
164	64 ½	16.0 ½
165	65	16.1
166	65 ¼	16.1 ¼
167	65 ¾	16.1 ¾
168	66 ¼	16.2 ¼
169	66 ½	16.2 ½
170	67	16.3
171	67 ¼	16.3 ¼
172	67 ¾	16.3 ¾
173	68	17.0
175	69	17.1
178	70	17.2
180	71	17.3

Minimum Height requirements per FHANA:
   150 cm or 14.3 hands for Studbook mare or gelding
   155 cm or 15.1 hands for star mare or gelding
   158 cm or 15.2 1/4 hands for model mare or 3 year approved stallion
   160 cm or 15.3 hands for 4 year approved stallion
Conversions:
   1 inch = 2.54 cm
   centimeters X .3937 = inches

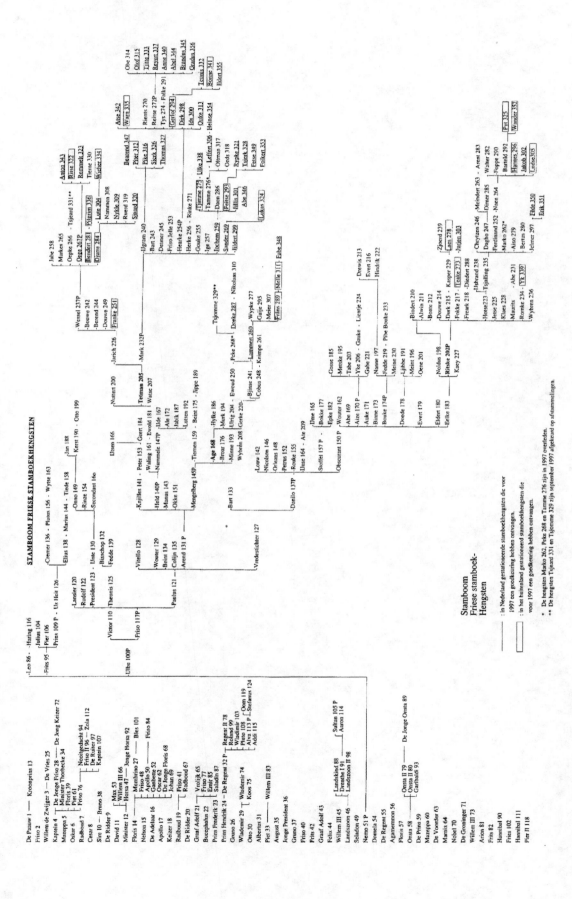

STAMBOOM FRIESE STAMBOEKHENGSTEN

Stamboom
Friese stamboek-
Hengsten

For the Love of the Friesian Horse

The author, Laura Beeman, is currently at work on her second book. "For the Love of the Friesian Horse", which is a compilation of art, photographs and stories that celebrate the eternal beauty of the Friesian horse. Submissions from Friesian owners and lovers are welcomed. If you have something you would like to submit, please contact the author via her website at: www.stoneywoodfriesians.com